Animal
HOMES

by E.K. Davis

illustrated by June Goldsborough

A GOLDEN BOOK · NEW YORK
Western Publishing Company, Inc., Racine, Wisconsin 53404

Animals live in lots of different places.

Birds live in nests.

Frogs live near ponds.

Bears live in caves.

A turtle's shell is its home.

Foxes live in dens under the ground.

Deer live in the forest.

Seals live on the ice.

A rabbit's home is called a burrow.

Squirrels live in hollow trees.

Fish live in the water.

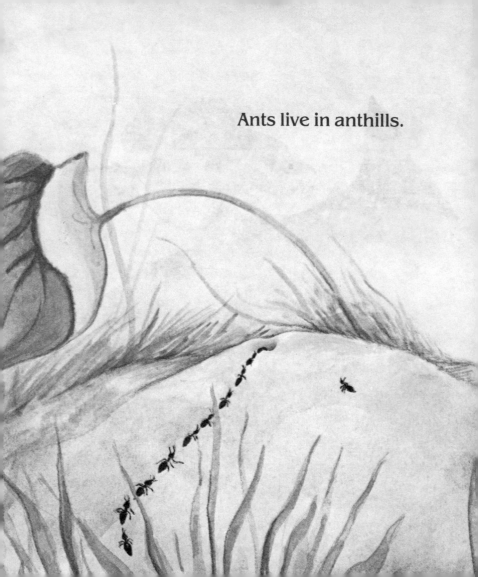

Ants live in anthills.

Puppies and kittens
live in houses with
people like you.